The Philosophy of Me

Dr. Christopher Everett

THE PHILOSOPHY OF ME

Copyright © 2014 Dr. Christopher Everett.

All rights reserved. No part of this book may be used or reproduced by any means, graphic, electronic, or mechanical, including photocopying, recording, taping or by any information storage retrieval system without the written permission of the publisher except in the case of brief quotations embodied in critical articles and reviews.

iUniverse books may be ordered through booksellers or by contacting:

iUniverse
1663 Liberty Drive
Bloomington, IN 47403
www.iuniverse.com
1-800-Authors (1-800-288-4677)

Because of the dynamic nature of the Internet, any web addresses or links contained in this book may have changed since publication and may no longer be valid. The views expressed in this work are solely those of the author and do not necessarily reflect the views of the publisher, and the publisher hereby disclaims any responsibility for them.

Any people depicted in stock imagery provided by Thinkstock are models, and such images are being used for illustrative purposes only. Certain stock imagery © Thinkstock.

ISBN: 978-1-4917-4115-3 (sc)
ISBN: 978-1-4917-4116-0 (e)

Library of Congress Control Number: 2014912430

Printed in the United States of America.

iUniverse rev. date: 10/30/2014

Prologue

Dr. Christopher Everett

My life's prayer

Lord,

Touch my head so that I may have wisdom

Touch my eyes so that I may see truth

Touch my ears so that I can hear your calling

Touch my back so that I may have strength

Touch my feet so that I will be steadfast

Touch my soul so that I may remain humble

Watch me on this day and protect me as I walk down the narrow road toward righteousness.

The Philosophy of Me

In the way of righteousness there is life;
along that path is immortality.

—Proverbs 12:28

Part 1

Reflection

This portion of the book shares a life concept that I have come to believe is in all of us. As we strive to live balanced individual lives, we strive also for balance in our relationships. If we can understand ourselves better and become balanced, then our relationships will benefit.

The Bliss Cycle

Through our travels in life we search for many things to aid us in being successful, such as companionship, education, career, and—most of all—money. These goals of success, if not balanced appropriately, can lead to unhappiness, insecurity, loneliness, or even regret. We prevent imbalance by actively pursuing balance. The achievement of balance creates a blissful experience that radiates from one's soul. The cliché "life happens" is true but how we respond to "life" dictates how we behave in the future.

I have found in my own life that once I achieve balance, I am soulfully happy. In short, I reached a state of bliss that radiated in everything I did and said. In life, nothing is ever perfect, and being blissful is no different. We may not ever achieve true bliss, which is synonymous with inner peace, but being close is better than not being close. I, like everyone, have had my share of ups and downs. Throughout this book, I will give you a glimpse into my life, including the highs, the lows, the emotion, and even the pain. All of these experiences have led me to the belief that bliss is real and possible.

What follows is my depiction of what we all will go through at some point in our lives. We all have experienced emotional events that made us feel completely out of control. Conversely, we have experienced periods in our lives in which we have dealt with people in an obtuse manner. Even worse, we have experienced hurt so deep that we intentionally acted in a manner that was inconsistent

The Philosophy of Me

with our core values. Often we first experience this hurt as anger. The reality is that, when someone is disrespected, mistreated, or taken advantage of, he or she becomes hurt emotionally. This hurt leads us to become manipulative, aggressive, and disrespectful toward others.

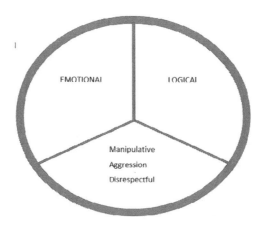

Everyone starts on either the emotional or logical side of the circle. When "life happens," it causes us to either become more emotional or more logical. In short, we slide further into the phase in life to which we are inclined at that moment. For example, stereotypically men are considered logical and practical which might cause them to miss the subtle emotional cues that women give off. When a man is emotionally hurt by a woman, he will generally fall down the slope of the circle and further away from being blissful. He may express his hurt by becoming more logical. He may say things such as "That makes no sense, so why should I do that?" In reality, many aspects of emotion and love make no sense but are the right thing to do.

The further away from bliss we move, the closer we are to an insane state of living. Have you ever heard the expression "There is a thin line between love and hate"? This is also true for those of us who are inclined to be logical. There is a thin line between logical behavior and being Manipulative, Angry, & Disrespectful (MAD) or HATE (Having Anger Towards Everyone).

After being hurt, our stereotypical man begins to look at life superficially in order to avoid dealing with his emotions. He is so far from emotion and balance (see diagram) that his actions become manipulative and subsequently disrespectful to others. He may view and treat women as objects rather than people. This is simply a protective mechanism from experiencing emotional hurt.

Do not think that women are exempt from this process of coping with hurt. They are human and just as fallible as men. Women experiencing hurt stereotypically start in the emotional phase and slide further from bliss in that direction. Then their actions become unstable because their emotions are erratic and, to an extent, unpredictable. Remember, there is a thin line between love and hate. Women's emotional states may tip toward being MAD or HATEFUL (having anger toward everyone feeling utterly lost).

Take a moment to reflect on your life or the life of someone close to you. What feeling or thoughts did you experience after being out of control emotionally? Depression, sadness, seclusion, regret, self-pity, embarrassment—the list goes on. These emotions are the expression of actions that were caused initially by hurt, but we are left holding the bag when we allow life to have its way.

The Philosophy of Me

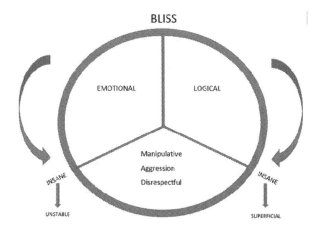

In the bliss cycle, no matter which way you enter, you can escape toward a blissful life in either direction. The stereotypical male will first have superficial and sexual escapades resulting in loneliness and regret. These regrets may be shared only with close friends or kept to himself. Then, as life as its irony, he may stumble across a woman he finds emotionally appealing. He may become infatuated with her and behave in a manner which contradicts his previously superficial lifestyle. He ultimately is on his way back to being blissful or balanced. After some time of this woman's positive affect on his life, he will start to become logically fixated on having a future with her. This balance between thought and emotion is the only reasonable explanation for why men purchase jewelry that sometimes takes months or years to pay off. The desire to please his woman creates a balance or bliss in the man's life that makes him want to wake up every day to be able to experience it over and over.

No matter which way you enter the bliss cycle, you can escape toward a blissful life in either direction. In our previous example of the stereotypical male, he entered the cycle in the logical phase, came through being MAD and ended up in the emotional phase. An individual may enter and exit through the same phase in which he or she started. A stereotypical female generally begins in the emotional phase, fantasizes in this phase, and ultimately this fantasy of sorts becomes her perceived reality. Many decisions that the woman makes are primarily based upon emotions or with the desire to obtain an emotional response. For example, our stereotypical woman who has been hurt might say things to her significant other in hopes that he will respond in a loving manner. Being balanced—or in a state of bliss—is crucial at this time. The woman's significant other might respond with actions that show love, but the woman may not interpret these actions as loving and ultimately reject them. She is blocked by emotions and fixated on what she needs or wants to receive. At some point she will confer with a trusted friend and seek her advice. Whatever advice she is given will start to pull her from a state of instability toward a state of bliss, but the entire time she is still "in her feelings." As her hurt subsides, she will work her way back toward a more blissful life.

When emotions are high, not only is the ability to receive others' actions as demonstrations of love more challenging; the ability to listen also becomes more difficult. When tempers are flared, our emotional filters are thicker, and we do not hear things as they are stated or sometimes intended. Just like a coffee filter, if the filter is too thick then we do not receive the important ingredient that we ultimately desire. If our hurt stereotypical woman has not received her significant other's actions as love, he finds himself at a loss and must explain himself and his love for her. If she is still hurt and has a lot of negative emotion, then she will be looking for particular words to heal her hurt. The man will try frantically to explain that his actions show love and his words are genuine. If her emotional filter is too thick, she will not hear him, resulting in sadness, disconnect, and hurt between the man and woman. This hurt leads to instability as both people now exist in a state of being MAD.

The Philosophy of Me

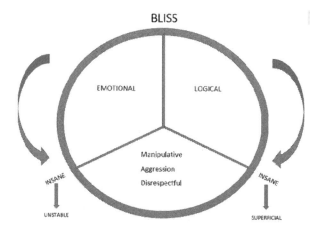

We have discussed our stereotypical male and how he may enter one side and exit the other. We also have discussed the stereotypical female and how she may enter the cycle and exit through the same. Both exits toward a more blissful life were prompted by a balance of what was lacking. For him he lacked emotions and emotions balanced his logic, while her emotions were balanced by the missing logic to help her heal. This recognition is important because as the bliss cycle is in all of us and exists in relationships as well.

Imagine, if you will, two separate cycles, one cycle predominant in emotion and another in logic. If these two cycles were to become one, for example in marriage, it is expected that they should balance each other out. In truth, they cancel each other out because the motivation for actions, words, or thoughts come from different places. Emotions are a powerful energy that can negate or neutralize the effects of logical or rational action or behavior. The practicality of logic does not always meet the expectations of or match the energy output of emotions. These opposing forces, if not managed appropriately, create an environment of separation. What was once two became one, and now one becomes two again. This is exemplified in many divorces in which one person is emotionally distraught and the other is calculating and cold.

If a man and woman are not near a blissful (balanced) state in their individual lives, then once they get together, things will continue in an unbalanced manner. Imagine the numbers of a clock placed around the cycle. In each phase of logic or emotion, there is a degree to how emotional or logical someone is. If one person is in the three o'clock position while another is in the ten o'clock position, they are far from balanced and unified as a unit. You may think that they offset each other or counter each other, but this couldn't be further from reality. If you have two powerful forces acting against each other, one must succumb to the other in order for there to be peace. Don't men give in to the emotions of women when they won't listen to logical reasoning? Don't women give into men and let them believe that they are right when everything they say is wrong? Once these two imbalanced circles are joined, the imbalance continues in their relationship. These two circles begin to pull in opposite directions. These counter forces become dangerous, with the potential to tear the singular circle of marriage back into the two separate individual circles. This is why it is important that both individuals are balanced in themselves before entering into a relationship.

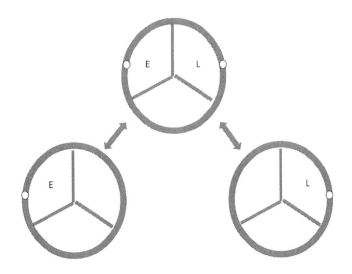

The Philosophy of Me

How do we ensure that we are able to reach a state of bliss within our individual self as well as our relationships? First, we must deal with ourselves and whatever issues that have kept us from being able to create balance within ourselves. Many of us ignore and subsequently make excuses for our behavior and constant poor judgment. As much as we try to run from ourselves, we cannot, and ultimately we lie to ourselves because we are afraid of ourselves. Here is a simple truth: Honesty leads to happiness. If one chooses to be honest with one's self about the areas one must improve to achieve balance, one can begin to be the best version of one's self. (I prefer not to use words such as "imperfections" or "flaws because words have associated connotations and those words also have power...Simple truth: It is easier to express negative thoughts than positive ones.)

This rebirth of self allows one to have a healthy relationship with another person. In a balanced state, we are able to be objective about ourselves. We are inclined to admit when we fall short because we now recognize the value in humility and respect the feelings of others. When we are able to show our partner this type of humility and love, we are able to bridge many gaps. This is not to say that healthy, balanced, or (my preferred term) blissful individuals will have a perfect life because no life is free of mistakes. But if we are content or blissful within ourselves, we begin to live on a higher plane of existence, minimizing pride, irrational actions, mood swings, deliberate attacks on others, and other egregious acts that hurt others and especially ourselves.

13

Part 2

Emotion

I poor my heart out and stand before you emotionally naked. Soulfully vulnerable to the impressions of life that are made. Yet, I am miraculously set free from the release that this openness has provided me.

Dr. Christopher Everett

Conversation with God

If God told me I could have one thing

It would not be for wealth or knowledge

It would not be for power amongst men

Nor fame with women

To have a fantastic career would not be my wish

But to know that you will be here for me and I for you

Because with that I need nothing else

The Philosophy of Me

Hope deferred makes the heart sick, but a
longing fulfilled is a tree of life.

—Proverbs 13:12

Dr. Christopher Everett

Early Morning Bloom

Two flowers bloom as the sun strokes the ground

Basking in all the sunlight that God has to offer

Even though they were soiled on jagged ground…
    they still bloom

Winters are long and cold beats at their petals…
    yet they still bloom

Heavy rain comes down and turns dirt into mud…
    and they still bloom

To the beat and song of a new day survival
    becomes a reality

With God by their side they will always bloom

The Philosophy of Me

And we know that for those who love God all things work together for good, for those who are called according to his purpose.

—Romans 8:28

Dr. Christopher Everett

Tornado

You came into my life like a Midwest whirlwind

In my mind I wanted nothing but to be friends

My heart began to melt after years of pain

A life changing event, none the less,
  that makes some go insane

I didn't want to love and thought it was over for me

I awake and realize that you are lying next to me

Smiles exchange, followed by a warm embrace

It is happening to me and all my fear is gone

The Philosophy of Me

For God gave us a spirit not of fear but of
power and love and self-control.

—2 Timothy 1:7

Dr. Christopher Everett

Untitled

Lost in thought and emotion while waiting
    to be whole again

Searching for a quiet night, one that has no end

"Have faith my friend" is faintly heard
    while standing in the watery abyss

Tattered cloth gently touches the back of his neck

Regret overwhelming from a love never found

Stays in his mind all the while in the hangman's noose

The Philosophy of Me

I have fought the good fight, I have finished
the race, I have kept the faith.

—2 Timothy 4:7

Dr. Christopher Everett

Athena's Daughter

Eyes cut left and then right

As she moves amongst the many faces

Her midnight hair flows to her shoulders

Eyes so beautiful, they put the sun to shame

When she smiles everything stops

As if God commanded us to look at his creation

She looks at me and my heart skips a beat

My mind is speaking but my mouth is not saying a word

I have seen Athena's daughter, but it is only a dream

For she lives with the gods, high above us mortals

The Philosophy of Me

Do not lust in your heart after her beauty
or let her captivate you with her eyes.

For a prostitute can be had for a loaf of bread
but another man's wife preys on your very life.

—Proverbs 6:25–26

Dr. Christopher Everett

Restoration

A simple hello has turned my life around

Her lips parted and my heart skipped a beat

Not out of fear or surprise but out of anticipation

I had been longing to hear her voice

To hear the sweet sound roll off her tongue

Shivers were sent down to the depths of my soul

Her voice touched me so deep that my soul orgasmed

It swirled thoughts and emotions that had been forgotten

Her lips, her voice stay in my ear

Now I am awake and my life is restored

The Philosophy of Me

Restore to me the joy of your salvation and
grant me a willing spirit, to sustain me.

—Psalm 51:12

Dr. Christopher Everett

Fingertips

I see her pass through the day and night

During the day she is the fantasy that
    would only be real in another reality

If you could see what I see then you would agree

She is absolutely phenomenal

A look into her eyes could melt a man's heart

Her radiant smile got me from the start

A touch of her hand, the sound of her voice

Could put a child to sleep

This woman is so fine; I would give anything
    to make her mine

So still she remains the light that brightens my day

And the fantasy that is still out of my reach

The Philosophy of Me

That each of you should learn to control your own body
in a way that is holy and honorable, not in passionate
lust like the pagans, who do not know God; And that
in this matter no one should wrong or take advantage of
a brother or sister. The Lord will punish all those who
commit such sins, as we told you and warned you before.

—1 Thessalonians 4:4–6

Dr. Christopher Everett

Intimate Delusion

Last night I had a dream

It seemed more like a fantasy

You were lying next to me dressed like a newborn baby

My hands rubbed your soft smooth skin

My lips touched you from head to toe and in between

I pleased you and you pleased me

A mind-blowing experience I couldn't conceive

Here you were bearing your innermost thoughts to me

Holding you close not with my hands but with my heart

We looked at each other with a sigh of relief

Knowing that we can fulfill each other's needs

I can't believe this is happening, can't believe you exist

But reality hits and you are not here

So that's what it will stay…just another dream

The Philosophy of Me

For though we walk in the flesh, we are not waging
war according to the flesh. For the weapons of our
warfare are not of the flesh but have divine power to
destroy strongholds. We destroy arguments and every
lofty opinion raised against the knowledge of God,
and take every thought captive to obey Christ.

—2 Corinthians 10:3–5

Dr. Christopher Everett

New Day

A breath of fresh air as the dust settles to the ground

The storm has passed, and the sun peeks around the clouds

Like a child peeking for Santa

The ground no longer shakes and the seas are calm

This is my life now…now that I have met you

The Philosophy of Me

For everyone who has been born of God overcomes the world.
And this is the victory that has overcome the world—our faith.

—1 John 5:4

Dr. Christopher Everett

Sunshine

I close my eyes and a light begins to shine

A warm feeling is in my chest

My stomach is no longer in knots but calm

The strength is back in my legs

Now I can overcome the darkness again

My heart sings the lover's song

I open my eyes and there we are

Wrapped in each other's embrace

Never wanting to let go

The Philosophy of Me

And Jesus answered them, "Have faith in God. Truly, I say to you, whoever says to this mountain, 'Be taken up and thrown into the sea,' and does not doubt in his heart, but believes that what he says will come to pass, it will be done for him. Therefore I tell you, whatever you ask in prayer, believe that you have received it, and it will be yours.

—Mark 11:22–24

Dr. Christopher Everett

Intimate Silence

Connected in her spirit is where he wants to be

Blinded by emotions that are uncontrolled and wild

Desirous of a love that the heavens know
how to provide

Waiting for that moment yet trying not to cry

Not from hurt or pain, but the reality has set in

Living on a cosmic plane while dying
on an empty earth

Reaching out to a place that only a few know exist

Reveling in the moment that her power
will be unleashed

Not trapped by the follies of humans
and their ignorance

But set free from that soul enduring speak

The one that takes place without a word
ever crossing one's lips

The Philosophy of Me

And above all these put on love, which binds
everything together in perfect harmony.

—Colossians 3:14

Dr. Christopher Everett

Missing Rib

It is a gift and a curse alike

Loving a woman that is

You feel on top of the world with your woman
    at your side

As you look at passers-by out the corner of your eye

Stupid in love is what she makes you feel

Sometimes more stupid than in love

Cloud nine is where her kisses cause you to reside

Or is it that you are so high,
    falling makes you feel as if it takes forever

Every time you see her you want
    to fall to your knees in praise

Right before the porcelain God at the end of the day

The Philosophy of Me

The thief comes only to steal and kill and destroy. I came that they may have life and have it abundantly.

—John 10:10

Dr. Christopher Everett

Carousel

Round and round his cerebellum spins in pain

Rat-ta-tat-tat is the sound that his heart makes

Night sweats consume his body and end a restless sleep

Anger has washed over him like crack in the hood

Moving down the block to the beat of a different tune

Not a heavenly one but the one that carries a devilish tone

Glazed over with all compassion taken away

Brown eyes fade to black, filled with an unending hatred

The desire to release this anguish is one phrase away

"Go get 'em" is the spinning chorus that flows in his dome

Unleash this fury no need not to share

To the ends of the earth and into the depths of hell

This is where his mind travels and his heart lies

Dr. Christopher Everett

The Pain of Love

Busy days give way to lonely nights

Lonely nights turn into unending pain

Pain so intense that the fires of hell cannot compare

A soul trembles with an uneven flow

Knowing of love that got away that is destined
to never return

A Spirit changed by a powerful force

Similar to the mountains being blown away
by Mother Nature's breathe

Tears fall and leave imprints of past mistakes
on a sorrowful soul

A mind lost in unending meditation gives way
to thoughts of releasing one's life

Life seems as though it is a blind man walking
in an open field

Every direction is a way toward freedom
but with every step he is still lost

The Philosophy of Me

Your hands fashioned and made me, and now you have destroyed me altogether. Remember that you have made me like clay; and will you return me to the dust? Did you not pour me out like milk and curdle me like cheese? You clothed me with skin and flesh, and knit me together with bones and sinews. You have granted me life and steadfast love, and your care has preserved my spirit.

—Job 10:8–12

Dr. Christopher Everett

The Morning Rose

How do you tell a rose it is beautiful if it will not open?

Sunlight shines upon it but it remains closed
    to the world

Inside, its bud is strong and secure

Safeguarded by its outer petals free
    from the turbulent world

The sun in all its might watches in awe
    of this tiny wonder

Begging to catch a glimpse of its beauty

Willing to shine its light forever if the rose will open

The Philosophy of Me

Be strong and courageous. Do not fear or be in
dread of them, for it is the Lord your God who goes
with you. He will not leave you or forsake you.

—Deuteronomy 31:6

Dr. Christopher Everett

Under the Full Moon

Two sets of pores vigorously entangled
  in a battle of superiority

Fighting the urge to submit to the other
  while both succumb to pleasure

Hips move to the sound of infantry man's snare drum

From the mountains to the valley, flood waters
  have been unleashed

Music is faintly heard while the eight-armed creature
  rises from the sunken abyss

United as one with the sole desire of endless ecstasy

Incestuous tirades are heard,
  reminiscent of the verbal berating of a slave

Simultaneously, punishment is laid as the organic rod
  is not spared

Images of erotic expression are seen
  as the two mirrors face another

Like the wolf at the full moon the majestic creature
  unleashes its call

A shadow of something wild and free now passes away

The waters are now calm and the two are no longer one

The Philosophy of Me

Beloved, I urge you as sojourners and exiles to abstain from the passions of the flesh, which wage war against your soul.

—1 Peter 2:11

Dr. Christopher Everett

Matching Piece

Sleepless nights are replaced by
a thought ridden mind of tranquility

A circulating angelic tone brings forth
a fledgling exuberance

Smiles place stake hold in a place
where few have been able to stay

A once feeble man's heart now rejoices
with a sun that shines through her eyes

The piece that was unknowingly gone
has now been replaced

A perfect fit in an imperfect existence makes living
easy to bear

Soulful death is laid to waste and peace
is at hand because of her

Pea-sized faith is what I fight to hold onto

For she is my peace, my matching piece,
but am I really hers?

The Philosophy of Me

Two are better than one, because they
have a good reward for their toil.

—Ecclesiastes 4:9

Dr. Christopher Everett

Sorrow

A seething sorrow courses through their veins

Not from a love lost but from a friendship slain

Romantic intentions twisted by words of the flesh

Hearts mistakenly vulnerable now lay confused
    and contorted

His promise of serenity is built like a Saharan oasis

Her words of truth are shrouded in a veil of fear

In the balance is a soul-quenching thirst for God's plan

Derailed by the inner workings of life's daily balance

Good and evil reign free, giving assuming hopes of safety

Yet no hopes have been born from the satisfyingly
    empty words of lovers

Minds set adrift while hearts seek continually
    for their equal

Souls without nourishment are left like slaves to starve

All while they lust for each other in disdain
    underneath the same star

The Philosophy of Me

But because of the temptation to sexual immorality, each man should have his own wife and each woman her own husband.

—1 Corinthians 7:2

Dr. Christopher Everett

Love's Cynicism

Pain is the only thing left

Joy has left his loving soul

Love has left his joyful life

Emotionally confused it what he remains

Is he meant to be alone?

Wounds have stopped bleeding but never healed

Pain has become his friend and anger his consolation

Loneliness becomes his guide as he walks in the darkness

His world, once bright, now seems to never shine

Except for a faint light that shines just as often as
    an eagle soars

Hope is nonexistent and his faith has dwindled

To God his back is not turned

But he is looking in the other direction

Life has created a cynical soul out of a loving spirit

The Philosophy of Me

Watch and pray that you may not enter into temptation.
The spirit indeed is willing, but the flesh is weak.

—Matthew 26:41

Dr. Christopher Everett

Supernova

My spirit cracked and my soul broke in two

Never thought that I could be feeling like this

My heart is racing and I can feel my pressure rise

The look in your eyes told me everything

But just like you I ignored what they were saying

A situation has occurred and it is small to some

My friend is heading for self-destruction

Concern has been mistaken for control

Decisions made in the blink of an eye
   has changed life forever

Do I stand by their side or stand by and cry

Shed tears for a person who I cannot help

Open watery gates in shame of having a broken heart

This is a supernova destroying everything in sight

So I stand by and shed a tear for my friend the supernova

The Philosophy of Me

For the time is coming when people will not endure sound teaching, but having itching ears they will accumulate for themselves teachers to suit their own passions, and will turn away from listening to the truth and wander off into myths.

2 Timothy 4:3–4

Dr. Christopher Everett

A Pale Light

Cold skin crawls with fear of life

The insides clench tight and hold on to a treasured gift

The barrier is high and the door is locked

Behind the door lie walls of stone

Beyond the rock there is darkness

It is the black sea ever flowing this way and that

In its midst lies a dull pale light

The light is dying as the wall grows higher

Its energy dissipates while the waters grow turbulent

Fear has won and all is lost

Hope is gone and without that there can be no love

The Philosophy of Me

Do not be anxious about anything, but in everything
by prayer and supplication with thanksgiving
let your requests be made known to God.

—Philippians 4:6

Dr. Christopher Everett

What I See

A fresh breath of ocean air as the sun rises
    to touch your face

A feeling so warm that it touches your soul

The sweetest strawberry touched with chocolate

The water rushing over your feet

While walking under God's light upon this dark earth

Now you understand what I see when you smile

I see something beautiful

The Philosophy of Me

Many women do noble things, but you surpass them all. Charm is deceptive, and beauty is fleeting; Honor her for all that her hands have done and let her works bring her praise at the city gate.

—Proverbs 31:29–31

Dr. Christopher Everett

Mind and Heart

Mentally you sit away and convince yourself
of what life is

Inside there is turmoil, a struggle of your very being

Never-ending tempest of life's most intimate fears

Denied emotional freedom, you are locked away
in the depths of your mind

Having peace within oneself is life's greatest struggle

Entering a place of rest to be on with the course life
takes you

Anger, confusion, and distrust have no place here

Remembering how you were once wrapped
in an embrace of happiness

To lose this is a tragedy, for many find it
but few will keep it

The Philosophy of Me

We are afflicted in every way, but not crushed;
Perplexed but not driven to despair; Persecuted but
not forsaken; Struck down but not destroyed.

—2 Corinthians 4:8–9

Dr. Christopher Everett

Eyes of a Sacred Soul

How do you trust when she has never been there?

Aphrodite spoke of love far more beautiful
    than the morning rose

She described a kiss so soft that the clouds
    would be shamed

Embraces so warm that Apollo would be envious

She told me of a delicate touch that could touch water
    yet keep it still

My soul has been lied to and my spirit remains crushed

My eyes see love no more

Sensitivity has left every inch of my body

Emotions have left my heart to be filled with nothing
    but anger

This life, this heart, this soul remains clouded forever

The Philosophy of Me

And above all these put on love, which binds
everything together in perfect harmony.

—Colossians 3:14

Dr. Christopher Everett

Lonely Nights

I sit away and a tear falls down my cheek

Lovely is a single heart

Happy is an awakened soul

I see you every night passing through my mind

Suddenly I awake but not from anxiety

But from an overwhelming feeling

To know that I will look in your eyes

And with one glance everything make sense

Just that thought keeps me lifted in the day

Yet keeps me still in the quiet of the night

The Philosophy of Me

I believe that I shall look upon the goodness of the Lord
in the land of the living! Wait for the Lord; be strong,
and let your heart take courage; wait for the Lord!

—Psalm 27:13–14

Dr. Christopher Everett

Two-Faced

I feel so weak and alone

One person helps me and comforts me

But another person hurts me

One holds me and tell me it is okay

The other pushes me away and berates me

While one touches my heart and kisses me softly

The other makes me feel worthless

One satisfies my every need

Unfortunately the other for me has no need

A loving embrace spawned into a fit of rage

A hug goodbye with a tear from my eye

Both of these are one in the same

The Philosophy of Me

I know your deeds, that you are neither cold nor hot. I wish you were either one or the other! So, because you are lukewarm—neither hot nor cold—I am about to spit you out of my mouth.

—Revelation 3:15–16

Dr. Christopher Everett

Anticipation

Sitting on the beach

The tide rolling onto my feet

Waiting for the sun to fall

The most beautiful sight I ever saw

Here it comes and there it goes

The wait is over but the yearning still goes on

Since the last time I saw you

And it's been some time

I'll see you soon, I just want to wait

But until that moment I'll be still and anticipate

The Philosophy of Me

Wait for the Lord; be strong, and let your
heart take courage; wait for the Lord!

—Psalm 27:14

Inside

A spot amongst the crowd

Loud screams fall on deaf ears

The pain exudes from every pore

Strong face hides all emotions

So tears have no place to fall except on the inside

Love once beautiful is now an ugly stain

It has withered away my soul and destroyed my heart

Where do you go when no one is there?

How do you cry when you have no tears?

Your heart breaks but it's too heavy for you to hold

Your spirit collapses and falls into an eternal abyss

Alone and scared with nothing to live for

Love has done something which knives could not

It has cut me in two and left me for dead

The Philosophy of Me

The plans of the heart belong to man, but the answer of the tongue is from the Lord. All the ways of a man are pure in his own eyes, but the Lord weighs the spirit. Commit your work to the Lord, and your plans will be established.

—Proverbs 16:1–3

Dr. Christopher Everett

Your Place

Looking at the space where your body once laid

The impression of your body still sunken
   in my resting place

A tear falls as the wells from my eyes open up
   on the inside

I feel you; your sin intertwined with mine

A tear falls; a loud silent scream shatters the walls
   of my heart

With closed eyes, your essence fills my lungs

Thoughts of your smile, visions of your face,
   memories of your kiss replay in my mind

Lingering and never-ending are my thoughts,
   my heart, and my love

The Philosophy of Me

More than that, we rejoice in our sufferings, knowing
that suffering produces endurance, and endurance
produces character, and character produces hope.

—Romans 5:3–4

Dr. Christopher Everett

Fade to Black

I open my eyes to blackness

A small shimmer of light blinds me

It is far away but still seems close

The crescent moon is out tonight

My hands sweat from an embedded nervousness

I feel an ominous presence floating in the air

I want to scream but my tongue cannot move

Weighed down by a dark force

Black magic has been cast against me

My feet are bolted down and fear is the shackle

Heart trembling yet fear wants to set me free

The crescent moon is moving away

That shimmer of light is getting closer

Nervousness is gone, fear has left

The magic has been lifted

I look at myself and no words are possible

I am sorry to those I left behind but now
   I am on my way

The Philosophy of Me

But to Jonah this seemed very wrong, and he became
angry. He prayed to the Lord, "Isn't this what I said, Lord,
when I was still at home? That is what I tried to forestall
by fleeing to Tarshish. I knew that you are a gracious and
compassionate God, slow to anger and abounding in love,
a God who relents from sending calamity. Now, Lord, take
away my life, for it is better for me to die than to live."

—Jonah 4:1–4

Internal Havoc

I sit and ponder on who, what, and why

Who is this person in my life?

What is happening inside of me?

Why do I feel the way I do?

All this emotion brings me so much pain

My insides toss and turn while my heart stays in turmoil

A supernova exists inside me and I fear I will lose my world

All because I decided to feel

Not feel as in a gentle touch from my hand to her face

But feel like the sensation from her warm embrace

Dazed and confused is all that I am

I know how to stop my pain just let go of her hand

Is that smart, is it even wise

How does a bird soar if first it doesn't fly

Now I am stuck, not between a rock and a hard place

But amid self-preservation and her warm embrace

The Philosophy of Me

Do not be conformed to this world, but be transformed by the renewal of your mind, that by testing you may discern what is the will of God, what is good and acceptable and perfect.

—Romans 12:2

Dr. Christopher Everett

Love's True Colors

As I sit, tears fall from my eyes

If you have ever been in love you know how death feels

To lose the one who makes your world go round

To not be with the person who can lift your spirits high

If love has crossed your path then
    you have looked death in the face

Should I give in or stay in my place

Tell death that I have lost but here I make my stand

I will rise through the pain for my love runs deep

Death will not conquer me for I am a survivor

I will not go until love has found me again

The Philosophy of Me

He will wipe away every tear from their eyes, and death shall
be no more, neither shall there be mourning, nor crying,
nor pain anymore, for the former things have passed away.

—Revelation 21:4

Dr. Christopher Everett

The Crow

I wake up in terror; bed wet from fear draining
out of my pores

Head pounding with thoughts of pain
and disappointment

What is that noise that I am hearing?

What I see is a picture being painted
in front of my eyes

A masterpiece in itself yet rubbish in my soul

The crow's exquisite sound flows
ever gently over my ears

In total discord my heart is left daily

My spirit longing for the masterpiece to end

As the sun breaks the lines of my eyes,
I see blackbirds sitting on my window sill

Knowing what is in my head, in my heart,
in my soul, I must fly with the birds

For in flight I am healed and my journey will go on

The Philosophy of Me

And after you have suffered a little while, the God of all grace, who has called you to his eternal glory in Christ, will himself restore, confirm, strengthen, and establish you. To him be the dominion forever and ever. Amen!

—1 Peter 5:10–11

Christopher Everett

Bathroom Mirror

Grotesque in nature, eyes with an unbearable pain

I am overcome with fear from the sight of it

It stared at me and me at it

I can feel it sucking my happiness away

An insulting grin placed upon his face

Anger rushed in and I yelled for it to go away

It disregarded my plea and began
   to peer into my soul

I feel it ripping my insides apart

My heart began to race and then it suddenly stopped

My soul began to bleed then there was no more

As I looked at this disgusting creature,
   its eyes glazed over

Its face was wet, but there was no rain

I trembled out of fear and stayed out of ignorance

What is this thing that fills me with disgust?

I blink once … I blink twice …
   It's just my bathroom mirror

The Philosophy of Me

After this, the word of the Lord came to Abram in a vision: "Do not be afraid, Abram. I am your shield, your very great reward."

—Genesis 15:1

Dr. Christopher Everett

History

Desperately, I long for you, trying in vain
    to catch the scent of you on the breeze

Diligently I put you out of my mind
    and back into my past … a distant memory

As the days go by you fade from the forefront
    of my thoughts

Your voice has become a whisper in my dreams

But just as the sea, I am pulled back under
    wishing you were here with me

All at once I long for you as if you were never mine

Though we both have moved on to different lives

I want nothing more than to turn back the time

To live you with my hands, my words, my actions,
    and not just with the quiet beating of my heart

The Philosophy of Me

He will wipe away every tear from their eyes, and death shall
be no more, neither shall there be mourning, nor crying,
nor pain anymore, for the former things have passed away.

—Revelation 21:4

Dr. Christopher Everett

Sinful Bed

Lying in the sanctuary ordained by God

Strangers at night dance with a hateful distance

Desiring for the other to succumb to humility

Longing for each other's gentle touch

The touch that precedes the exhale of an anger released

Pride has created this distance and Satan is the tailor

The potter has spun his wheel and waits
    for his clay to soften

For his hands create masterpieces
    that cannot be undone …

The Philosophy of Me

Let marriage be held in honor among all, and
let the marriage bed be undefiled, for God will
judge the sexually immoral and adulterous.

—Hebrews 13:4

Dr. Christopher Everett

The Light

Trapped in a place where pain reigns free

A troubled soul fights to stay alive

Followed by hurt and blinded by lies

It is weary and tired wanting all the hurt to subside

Partaking in an eternal sleep would stop this pain

But there is a ray of light that shines, brief but bright

It shows this tormented soul that there is life left

That if he chooses to fight the good fight

The light, will find its way back

And it will never leave and always brighten

The world of this disturbed heart

The Philosophy of Me

May the God of hope fill you with all joy and peace in believing, so that by the power of the Holy Spirit you may abound in hope.

—Romans 15:13

Passion

An unquenchable desire that gently pushes forward

Pulls energy from deep within to show
the world its beauty

Sleepless nights are welcomed to the tune
of melodic sounds

Pain from life's setbacks are deflected
with a choosing of a higher perspective

Love can't compare to the waves in which
she has caused me

Strong powerful and never to be ended
even when God calls you home

Nourishment isn't needed to feed my soul
for she provides all of my needs

I am blessed to know her and without shame
proclaim my love for her

She is what has given me success and kept me
from the hurt I once felt.

I pray you experience this … I pray you find your passion!

The Philosophy of Me

Whatever you do, work heartily, as for
the Lord and not for men.

—Colossians 3:23

Dr. Christopher Everett

Arise

Forged in the ashes I am arisen in a blaze

Like a phoenix majestic and powerful,
I am designed for greatness

Not from krypton but stepping to me
wrong will get you rolled on

God-given strength with a passion burning
like an Olympic torch

Not moving and shaking because "train"
is my middle name

Failure is a setback to some but to me
it is an opportunity to learn

Perspective like Darwin…I am ever evolving

Mind like where's Waldo…I am ever searching

Moving toward success then onward toward more

Not for the money and to hell with fame

But simply for the love of it

The Philosophy of Me

But you are a chosen race, a royal priesthood, a holy
nation, a people for his own possession, that you
may proclaim the excellencies of him who called
you out of darkness into his marvelous light.

—1 Peter 2:9

Dr. Christopher Everett

Her

To have her wrapped in a celestial embrace of protection

This is my desire for her

To insert myself inside her with no sexual intent

Breathing me as I breathe her knowing destiny
    is fulfilled with each rise and fall of our chests

Wanting her to believe in her mind
    that she is the best for me

Not because of my own understanding but
    because I have leaned on God's

On my knees I pray for her pain to be given to me

I will carry her burden; I will fight her fight

So that she can live free and no longer be blinded

To the love that I know she has for me

The Philosophy of Me

Nevertheless, in the Lord woman is not independent of man nor man of woman.

—1 Corinthians 11:11

Dr. Christopher Everett

Kool-Aid Smile

On a routine chance meeting I met the woman
   life intended for me

Trapped by morality and bound by obligation
   our conversation stayed superficial

My spirit was moved and begged to be set free

Thoughts went every which way but straight,
   plotting against what was supposed to be in my heart

Laughable demeanor with a Kool-Aid smile,
   all the while my insides stirred

My chance conversation turned into permanent
   contemplation

Nostalgia takes over as dreams of fantasized happiness
   now seem possible

In her there is no doubt—there is no shame—
   the life which has given her pain is now gone

Her eyes show love, her face gives delight,
   and her soul longs to be held

Lord, help push me; give me the answer to this prayer,
   for all I dream of is holding her soul

The Philosophy of Me

He who finds a wife finds a good thing
and obtains favor from the Lord.

—Proverbs 18:22

Dr. Christopher Everett

Our Space

Not just physically but spiritually

I miss making love to you endlessly

The type of lovemaking that precedes
the bedroom behavior

The kind that hours after you still savor

Your hands on my back

My mouth on your tongue

Our gazes locked on each other

In that place there is no fear, no insecurity, just
a safe haven where nothing else exists but our love

The Philosophy of Me

There is no fear in love, but perfect love casts out fear. For fear has to do with punishment, and whoever fears has not been perfected in love.

—1 John 4:18

Dr. Christopher Everett

Dread

Dueling hemispheres partake
   in an inconsistent exchange of thought

Soul peering spheres are cracked open
   and unleash their turmoil

Covered by the soothing nature
   of a perfect innocence

Still mental exchanges give way
   to the tempest that is at hand

Harmonious blessings are received,
   intermingled with a dreadful silence

A bone-chilling breeze seizes control of
   warm hearts once beating in unison

The shuffling of reaper's feet echoes
   in the mind's eye of clouded judgment

The promise of a new day gives him
   pleasure as he continues his torment

The Philosophy of Me

For the perfect innocence has shunned his presence
 and welcomes his child no more

Holding the beautiful black cloak, marching toward
 a dreary beginning

Afraid no more of what is to come but fearful of
 not knowing what is behind

Loved ones left with clear confusion and
 delectable disdain for answers unknown

Good-byes are yelled at the loudest pitch
 but nothing is returned

For the path ahead respect nothing
 of love and only feeds of pain and dread

To the married I give this charge (not I, but the Lord): the
wife should not separate from her husband but if she does,
she should remain unmarried or else be reconciled to her
husband, and the husband should not divorce his wife.

—1 Corinthians 7:10–11

Dr. Christopher Everett

Destructive Truth

Flawlessly arrogant your imperfections you never speak

Uncomfortable silence screams of displeasure
between fear and fearless

Coincidently lustful love becomes poison to the senses

Killing ever so slowly the power that
was once awakened within

Yearning for the bond that was promised from our father

Only to find that life was more like a bad trip on molly

Ultimately anger sets in and fuses to your spine

Hardly letting go, relentlessly infecting your soul

Astoundingly astonishing is the pitfall of trust

Rudimentary feelings mixed with sophomoric intellect

Destroyed the one last hope … Yes, love did the damage

The Philosophy of Me

The reward for humility and fear of the
Lord is riches and honor and life.

—Proverbs 22:4

Part 3

Wisdom

I have never been the smartest one, but I have used God's blessing of insight to learn valuable lessons that have sustained me through my trials and humbled me in my success.

I Am Strong

I am strong …not because I move small mountains but because I have been battle tested. Vested are my interests in the one who sits the highest. He has placed me on a shelf of power and crowned me with his wisdom. Grace has been given to me and mercy bestowed. I do not proclaim, "Get behind me, Satan," for he knows his place at my Lord's feet. Now I have been exalted by the most highest. The serpent king sits beneath my feet as well. The gates of hell have prevailed at receiving its defeat … for I am not just powerful beyond measure but infinitely miraculous.

I am tremendously blessed with God's forgiveness for withholding this gift is death upon one's self. The festering of hate seeps into one's soul when one cannot let pain go. Love pain, life pain, self-inflicted all creates wounds but infinite mercy and unquestionable forgiveness heal. I am strong … not because my stature resembles the body of a Greek warrior statue, but because I have been given an indomitable will to stay the course. I have honed my ability to focus with the lessons God has allowed me to encounter. Like a hawk searching for prey, I am such in my life narrowing in on my goals. Perfection will always be out of my grasp but the pursuit of it will always be my task.

I am strong … not because I can bellow for miles upon miles but because I accept God's role for me. I humble myself to his will and stand at his side; "helper" is what he calls me with the will to receive others' pain, the ability to churn their sorrows into

The Philosophy of Me

moments of freedom to give glimpses of a happiness promised to us all. I boast not of what I have done I just share what has been done for me. He has charged me to pay it forward, not pay it back. He has commanded that I stay in my place and do his will until he calls me home.

I am strong, for I accept his humility as my mission. I am strong because I have the power to kneel at his feet and not stand with my chest high. I am amazing because he says so. I am anointed because he has ordained it. I am no longer afraid of the dark because light leads my way ... I see him, he sees me ... I am in him, and he is in me ... I love my God, and he loves me. That's why I am strong!

War Machine

Every war is preceded by a conflict. It is a conflict of ideals that are so far different that their very existence together is an abomination. God knows this and crafted his angels to protect those who stand for the beliefs that are breathed from his own very mouth. He crafted these individuals and laid them on a path as to where they grew into soldiers for the war. They aren't designed to start or finish the war but molded to stand up in times of war. Their watch word is "faith," and their creed is "I will not run from chaos nor run to it. I will not lay down but I will stand up in the midst of the storm. For those who aren't able, I will remain capable. And for Him, my Lord is the only one to whom I shall kneel!"

War machines, like the slogan says… these people, are built God tough! Able to withstand the pressures of life while being compassionate to those who are downtrodden in their strife. Willing to shield others from the venom of the serpent king, with willful disregard for their own safety. They gladly take the venom meant for others into their veins because God filled them with the antidote. War machines are powerful beyond measure, with a strength that puts the titans of Olympus to shame. Blessed with insight and X-ray vision in order to see who is sincere and who is just playing with God's religion. The battles they fight take a toll on their spirits. Like Job they will fall ill and broken, appearing to be slain. But as God told Satan, "On him, do not lay a finger." Their fight is long and everlasting, but the lives they save are protected from the collateral damage of pain. War

The Philosophy of Me

machines speak life into people and never take it away. Even for their enemies they still find time to over them pray. Their capacity to carry other's hurt runs deep like the abyss of the sea...endless, at least to most. A presence so recognizable that when they leave, a subtle emptiness occurs. Yet joy is left behind as well.

These people are special creatures, yet they are very plain. They are around us daily, and we even know their names. They know their worth but speak of themselves as if they were poor. They see the good in all that is rotten just to remind others that hope is never forgotten. Their walk, their talk, their gaze, and their words are nothing like you have heard before. They possess a resilience and intelligence that causes weak-minded people to cry out in shame. They are detested by the cowards and plotted on by the lame. For the war machines, God has all the glory, for they are vessels of his greatness and provide living testimonies in his name. If you find one, use one, accept from them everything ... because you never know how quickly they will be gone until they are on the very next plane.

Chris's Food for Thought

- Don't allow your emotionality to outweigh your morality!
- Compassion begets listening; listening provides perspective; perspective increases wisdom. Have you tried some compassion today?
- Observing people's words and actions is a lost art. People will tell you who they are and if you matter. If you just observe, you will find this to be true. But you must speak to confirm what you have observed, and once silence is given as your answer … you then know the truth.
- Holding a grudge is justifying your inability to forgive. If you know a person's heart, know he or she will make mistakes.
- For some people, telling a lie is like a fart. They do it and think nobody knows it happened.
- The only thing that stands between you and success is effort and energy!
- Excuses are just a reason for people to accept failure.
- Distorted or hidden truths are the expression of a person's insecurities.
- Faith is endeavoring into something with hope but not knowing how it will work out. Don't allow negative perceptions and negative assumptions to bind your faith. Just leap!
- Love the way God intended, with a selfless and enduring commitment and the will to care about and benefit another person by righteous, truthful, and compassionate thoughts, words, and actions.

The Philosophy of Me

- Only two people can tell you to quit. God won't do it, so why should you?
- Sometimes getting respect is a simple matter of you leaving a disrespectful situation.
- I wake up and choose to live ... I live to love ... I love to live!
- Honesty leads to happiness.
- Love is the inconvenience of oneself for the benefit of others.
- Real love is a soul-changing experience that purposes the heart and directs the mind!

Testimony

I have come a long way and made many mistakes along life's way. I attribute all my success to God and my failures to my own free will. But I have been blessed to be given the opportunity to learn from my heartache, bad decisions, misguided direction, and most of all, my sin. He has blessed me to be able to live vicariously through close friends and family, whose experiences have helped shape my frame of mind and ultimately these thoughts.

I will never be perfect, but I live in the continual pursuit of being the best me. Many people along the way have pushed me to write. I couldn't see the blessing in their encouragement because I ignored my own hurts which bound my initiative. The hurts turned into fears, and the fears turned into excuses. Ignoring the pain never allowed me to face the hurts in order to heal my wounds, create balance in my life, and be the best me. I allowed hurt and excuses to bleed into my relationships, not only with women but with my family and friends as well. My self-righteous hurt was a badge of honor that I used to justify my wrongness. The hurt kept me alone when I most needed someone. I am no longer that man, but I am destined to be what God has called me to be: a helper for his people. I was not able to fulfill his purpose for me because I was blind, but now I am me!

I pray that these words bring you insight and provide you with a different perspective. This philosophy can always be debated because there is no one right way to be mentally, emotionally, or

The Philosophy of Me

spiritually healthy. I strongly believe in the ideas in this book and prescribe to them daily. Even when I fall short, I open myself up to the Lord and allow him to bring me back to a state of bliss. May God keep you...Thank you!

Made in the USA
Middletown, DE
18 June 2019